Heeling
the Canine
Within

Heeling the Canine Within

A Dog's Self-Help Companion

ILLUSTRATIONS BY
LIANE LESHNE

Max and Scooter

BALLANTINE BOOKS

NEW YORK

A Ballantine Book
Published by The Ballantine Publishing Group

http://www.randomhouse.com

Library of Congress Cataloging-in-Publication Data

Leshne, Liane.
    Heeling the canine within : a dog's self-help companion / Max
& Scooter ; [Liane Leshne and Sharon Armstrong]. — 1st ed.
        p.   cm.
    ISBN 0-345-42201-5 (alk. paper)
    1. Dogs—Humor.   I. Armstrong, Sharon.   II. Title.
PN6231.D68L47   1998
818 .5407—dc21   98-14361
                                                         CIP

Text Design by H Roberts Design
Cover design by Ruth Ross

Illustrations by Liane Leshne

Manufactured in the United States of America

First Edition: July 1998

10 9 8 7 6 5 4 3 2 1

Max's dedication:

To my grandfather, Robert Leshne, and to the memory of my adoring grandmother, Renée Leshne, who always said, "I am *not* grandmother to a dog," but who spoiled me pretty good anyway.

Scooter's dedication:

For my dad, Richard Armstrong; my grandmother, Margaret Scott; and my two godmothers, Irene Cardon and Allyn Gutauskas.

Heeling the Canine Within

Introduction

*P*eople think they're the only ones with problems: work problems, relationship problems, eating problems—you name it. But what about us? We're the ones who have to *listen* to all these problems and keep wagging our tails when the day is done. Sadly, this can lead to "empty wagging." Take our friend Jake. He got to feeling so bad about his owner's poor investment decisions that he stopped eating for a week. And Bucky chewed up an entire drawer of underwear when his owner got dumped. You probably know of a similar story.

That's why we decided it was time for a self-help book for dogs. People have books telling them how to eat, how to think, even how to breathe properly. We think it's our turn, so we offer this guide to recapturing the puppy within you—call it a little Rawhide for the Soul.

One caveat before you begin, though. Please remember—we're not licensed therapists, we're just licensed dogs.

Happy reading.

S.N.I.F.F.
(Standardized Neurosis Inventory for Fido)

ark the response that best matches your behavior.

1. You have just broken the owner's favorite ceramic vase. You:
   (a) Run into another room and hide
   (b) Cultivate a pitiful expression and hope for sympathy
   (c) Attempt to rearrange the pieces into a decorative mosaic of *The Last Supper*

2. The owner buys you a new collar. You:
   (a) Wear the new collar
   (b) Refuse to part with the old collar
   (c) Worry that wearing the new collar may imply too much of an emotional commitment

3. You and the owner are taking a drive. You:
   (a) Sit quietly and enjoy the scenery
   (b) Hang out the window with your tongue out
   (c) Wonder if you are a safe distance from the air bag

4. You've just had an accident on the rug and the owner has called you a "bad dog." You:
   (a) Slink away remorsefully
   (b) Growl defiantly
   (c) Blame your father for having abandoned you at birth

5. The owner goes into McDonald's and leaves you in the car because a county health ordinance prohibits dogs in eating establishments. You:
   (a) Silently pray for fries
   (b) Silently pray for Chicken McNuggets
   (c) Consider forming a separatist movement to overthrow the government

6. You're walking with the owner when a stranger points at you and says, "My, he looks just like Rex." You:
   (a) Wonder who Rex is
   (b) Ignore the comment and keep on walking
   (c) Worry that you may have fathered some puppies in another county

7. During your last day at the kennel, you:
   (a) Keep a low profile
   (b) Exchange addresses with the other dogs
   (c) Start a support group

8. You learn that one of your relatives has just been taken to the pound. You:
   (a) Send a sympathy card
   (b) Organize a rescue party
   (c) Call Alan Dershowitz

9. Some of your friends are sensing an impending earthquake. You:
   (a) Run like hell
   (b) Warn the owner
   (c) Carry a sign saying "The End Is Near"

10. The pooper scooper law has just been passed. You:
   (a) Hope the owner complies
   (b) Order a deluxe model
   (c) Practice biofeedback to control your bodily functions

11. Analyze the following inkblot and mark the response that most closely fits the image you see:
   (a) Monday's accident on the Ralph Lauren comforter
   (b) Tuesday's accident on the antique Persian rug
   (c) The cat and its evil twin

Total up the number of "c" responses. If you have more than five, *chew up this book and digest the contents.*

1
Realize That Accidents Will Happen
(and Learn to Camouflage Them)

*T*here is no reason to beat yourself up over an occasional Accident. The owner will be mad enough for both of you. And most important, it is often through Accidents that we learn. Consider how our ancestors tried to make creative use of their surroundings.

The Stone Age

The art of camouflage was not so easy during the Stone Age. When a cave dog had an Accident, there was no furniture to hide it under, so when the owner came home, there was the Accident staring him in the face. (On the other hand, there were no Persian rugs, so the owner wasn't likely to be too upset. And was it such a big deal if the owner *did* become upset? Let's face it—being forced to sleep outside wasn't much worse than being allowed to sleep inside.)

The Middle Ages

Dogs in the Middle Ages had lots of gigantic furniture to work with, but the basement was filled with such hideous torture devices that no dog was ever willing to risk it.

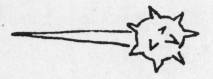

The Victorian Era

Dogs fared much better in the Victorian Era, when rooms were cluttered with lots of rococo chairs and harpsichords, and Accidents could go unnoticed for years. By the time the owner noticed the Accident, everyone in the household had either died, been married off, or gone insane.

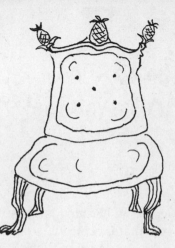

The Twentieth Century

Anything goes, and it's all a matter of décor. If your owner's tastes are minimalistic—say, Danish modern—you must be creative. Good targets are **(1)** recently watered plants, **(2)** exercise equipment the owner used once and forgot about, and **(3)** a spot behind the futon. (For more ideas, pick up a copy of *Architectural Digest*.)

2
Break the Cycle of Passive-Aggressive Chewing

*P*assive-aggressive chewing is a manifestation of anger at the owner that is rooted in separation anxiety. The owner has selfishly stayed out late drinking with coworkers. In the meantime, you have compulsively eaten two-thirds of the couch and several decorative pillows for good measure. (It is no excuse that the pillows were insufferably ugly.)

This behavior is not only hard on the digestive system but potentially self-destructive, as it poses the risk of your being confined to a less luxurious room of the house next time the owner is away. (See also *Breaking the Crates That Confine*.)

Here are some effective relaxation techniques that can help us break the cycle of passive-aggressive chewing:

Positive affirmations

Too often, anger at the owner is really a manifestation of deeper-rooted feelings that we somehow do not deserve the owner's love. We may have heard one too many times that we are bad dogs and come to believe this.

Try replacing the following negative beliefs with these positive affirmations:

Negative belief: "I am a bad dog. *Bad dog!*"
Positive affirmation: "I am a good boy. *Good boy!*"

Negative belief: "I have fleas."
Positive affirmation: "I am a gracious host to many other life forms."

Negative belief: "I am not as good as the cat."
Positive affirmation: "The cat is not fit to lick my paws."

Aromatherapy

Though relatively new to Western dogs, this relaxation technique has actually been practiced for thousands of years by Chinese canines. Scents we have found most soothing are **(1)** several-days-old garbage, **(2)** road kill, and **(3)** any substance the owner spilled behind the refrigerator several months ago and forgot about. (But the possibilities are endless, of course.)

If these techniques fail and you find yourself heading for the decorative pillows, take a deep breath and chase your tail for 30 seconds. This really works!

3
End Obsessive-Compulsive Scratching

*T*he problem here is that scratching feels so *good* that many of us find we are unable to stop. While this may seem like a harmless diversion, the danger is that, inevitably, the owner catches us and we end up in the tub. Try the following creative visualization exercise to end obsessive-compulsive scratching:

1. Sit quietly in the middle of the room staring at nothing in particular. (Just like you were doing a few minutes ago.)
2. Close your eyes and empty your mind of all conscious thought. (Just like the cat is doing right now.)
3. Imagine that you are rolling in soothing, fishy-smelling mud.
4. As you envision the mud coating your body, say to yourself, "I have no need to scratch. The mud is all I need."

(For more on affirmations, see *You'll Smell It When You Believe It: The Power of Positive Stinking*.)

Incidentally, if the worst happens and you *do* end up in the tub, be sure to give a good shake coming out, soaking the owner and as much of the surrounding area as possible. This technique leaves the owner thinking, "Thank God we don't have to do *this* more than once or twice a year." (See also *Owners Who Bathe Dogs and the Dogs Who Love Them*.)

4

Avoid Tennis Ball Dependency

*T*he key here is to understand that there are any number of toys that can make us happy. By focusing too much attention on any one toy we run the risk of developing Tennis Ball Dependency.

Consider the example of our unfortunate Lab friend, Jed, who developed a fierce attachment to one particular tennis ball. One day, the owner found the tennis ball had become so repellent that she unceremoniously disposed of it. Jed is now in therapy trying to deal with the loss.

The best way to avoid Tennis Ball Dependency is to make sure the owner provides a steady stream of new toys. Follow this simple, two-step program:

1. Play with a new toy for *one week only*.
2. At the end of that time, no matter how much you are enjoying the toy, bury it, or "lose" it under the bed or behind the couch. (It is also effective to sigh and glance at the toy with a disappointed expression when you know the owner is looking.)

By abandoning toys regularly, you send the message that your toys are simply not interesting enough and must be replaced by other, more interesting ones. You can amass an impressive collection this way and, more important, avoid the trap of Tennis Ball Dependency. (See also *Simple Abundance of Tennis Balls*.)

5

Live Down the Lassie Complex

Okay. So Lassie rescued Timmy whenever he fell down the well. Big deal.

You should never be intimidated by Lassie, for two reasons. First, for dogs, Cute is much more important than Smart. Second, unless you live in a rural area, how likely is it that your owner is going to fall down a well? Owner problems today are far more complex. When the owner has just been cited for violating securities laws, it's much more important to curl up next to the owner and look cute than it is to run back and forth barking.

6

Stop Chasing Cars
(and Other Hints on
Realistic Goal-Setting)

Since we have been chasing things on wheels since before the beginning of organized agriculture, you may ask why this behavior is considered self-destructive. After all, our ancestors most certainly chased The Wheel, and you may even have a grandmother who caught an Edsel once.

The problem is that, in trying to live up to the reputation of our ancestors, we find ourselves pitted against supercooled, turbo-charged engines and Pirelli tires. This is a battle we simply cannot win, with or without Nikes. (You know the truth in this if you have ever tried to catch a Lexus or, still worse, a sport utility vehicle.)

Understand that sometimes success lies in redefining our goals. Chase something slower, like the neighbor's fat Siamese. Or, better yet, forget about chasing altogether and take up something new, like learning to work the doorknob or designing your own Web page.

If you find you must chase something on wheels, stick
to people on bicycles delivering pizza.

7

Confront Your Feelings of Mixed-Breed Inadequacy

Every year a bunch of dogs with long, hyphenated names meet at Madison Square Garden, where their owners trot them around in circles for two nights until one is declared the "winner." Sure, these dogs are sleek and beautiful; sure, they have great teeth

and sparkling personalities; and sure, they will probably earn more in two nights than you ever will in your whole life. But ask yourself: Outside of a runway in

Atlantic City, do great teeth and a bubbly personality really matter?

The point is, these dogs have absolutely no street-smarts and couldn't find the back of a garbage truck if it hit them in the face. (To say nothing of the inbreeding issue.) If you are a mixed-breed, be proud! Heinz 57 goes a lot farther in this world than Grey Poupon. (See also *I'm Okay, You're a Mutt*.)

8
Stop Burying the Past
(and Digging It Up Again)

 e all have things we like to keep buried. The conventional wisdom is that we will feel better if we bring these things out into the open. This can be a big mistake.

Case Study

You have seized one of the owner's Amalfi pumps, chewed off the heel (See chapter 2, "Break the Cycle of Passive-Aggressive Chewing"), and buried the remaining piece in the yard. Several days later, acting on a wayward impulse, you dig it up and decide to carry it around the house for a while, and possibly leave it sitting on the piano bench for the owner to admire.

The owner, who was looking for the Amalfi pumps that morning, is not as pleased as you are with the result. Within seconds, you hear the dread rhetorical question "WHAT DID YOU DO?" (See chapter 14, "Read Your Owner Like a Book.") You are now in big trouble. Your only hope at this point is to find the mate, convert both shoes into open-toed sandals, and return them to the closet in the hope that they will be appropriate for dress-down Friday. (This strategy is risky, however, if the owner thinks open-toed sandals make her ankles look thick.)

It is much better to leave the past buried. If you are unable to do this, stick to old Keds.

9
Get Adopted in 21 Days

*T*his chapter is for shelter dogs who are waiting to get adopted. There are proven techniques for getting picked by the owner of your choice—and for avoiding bad owners. The first step is distinguishing the good ones from the bad. Study the following profiles:

Good Owner Profile
- Smiling
- Wearing comfortable walking shoes
- Saying things like "Oh, my, doesn't he look underfed?" (Bonus points for Big Mac on the breath.)

Bad Owner Profile
- Wearing fatigues and a flak jacket but is not in the military
- Saying things like "This one looks pretty tough" while checking your teeth
- Discussing whether you will live inside or outside "the compound"

Once you've become familiar with the profiles, it's only a matter of adopting the correct behavior. If you see a potential owner you like, do the following:

1. Jump up and place your front paws on the kennel bars.
2. Wag your tail voraciously.
3. Make eye contact.
4. Try not to scratch too much (although a little scratching is okay if it makes you look more pitiful).

Conversely, if you see a potentially *bad* owner eyeing you, exhibit the following behavior:

1. Go to the far end of the kennel and sit facing the wall.
2. Howl a little in a way that says, "I'll be doing this late at night."
3. Scratch incessantly.
4. Hum "Feelings" (but be careful—this may also drive away good owners).

After you've been adopted, be sure to establish the ground rules early on, because bad habits are hard to break. Make sure the new owner understands right from the beginning that you will be sleeping in the bed, that you will be allowed on the furniture, and that you are entitled to at least half of any Chinese food that is delivered. Also, make it clear that small children and overnight guests will be tolerated, but only to the extent that they are well behaved. Otherwise, they will have to go.

10
Avoid the Agony of Owner-Inflicted Cross-Dressing

*T*his pertains to small male dogs whose owners think it is acceptable for them to wear little bows and ribbons. We have known many Yorkies, Malteses, and poodles who have a bad reputation for irritable barking. This has nothing to do with temperament; it is a direct result of owner-inflicted cross-dressing, which produces limitless inner anguish. Under no circumstances should bows or ribbons be tolerated.

If the owner tries to place a ribbon on your head, immediately swipe it off with your front paw. The owner may be persistent. *You* be persistent. Ribbon. Swipe. Ribbon. Swipe. Eventually, the owner will tire of this and turn to something simpler, like redecorating the living room. (This will also provide a fresh supply of decorative pillows.)

11
Discover the Hidden Messages in Your Dreams

f you've read *Freud for Dogs*, you know that you can learn a great deal from your dreams—especially since you probably spend at least 16 to 20 hours a day sleeping. Here are some common interpretations.

Cars

If you dream about chasing a car, this may be a sign that you are setting unrealistic goals and need to reassess your priorities. (See chapter 6, "Stop Chasing Cars.")

If you dream about chasing a car and catching it, you are probably experiencing feelings of high self-esteem. (If you dream about chasing a Brinks armored truck, however, be careful. You may be harboring criminal tendencies.)

If you dream about chasing a little red sports car, you may be approaching middle age.

Cats

If you dream about chasing a cat, you are angry at something. (Probably the cat.)

If you dream about a cat hissing at you, you are facing some kind of unresolved conflict. (Probably the cat hissing at you.)

If you dream about chasing and capturing a cat, forget it. This is pure wish fulfillment.

Shedding

If you dream that you are shedding, you may be internalizing your owner's fear of male-pattern baldness. Try a little Rogaine before bed.

Squirrels

This is a recurring dream among city dogs. If you dream about chasing squirrels, you are probably experiencing an unconscious desire for greater freedom than your condominium lifestyle permits.

Teeth and Biting

If you dream that your teeth are falling out, you may be feeling guilty about having eaten the owner's Amalfi pumps. (See chapter 8, "Stop Burying the Past and Digging It Up Again.")

If you dream about biting the hand that feeds you, this indicates serious self-destructive tendencies. Seek help immediately.

Treats

If you dream about treats, congratulations. You are not sexually repressed or hopelessly neurotic. You are just a well-adjusted dog. (It is also possible that you and the owner are having the same dream.)

The Vet

If you dream about visiting the vet, you are having a nightmare. Your only hope is to wake up as fast as possible. (See chapter 13, "Face Your Fears.")

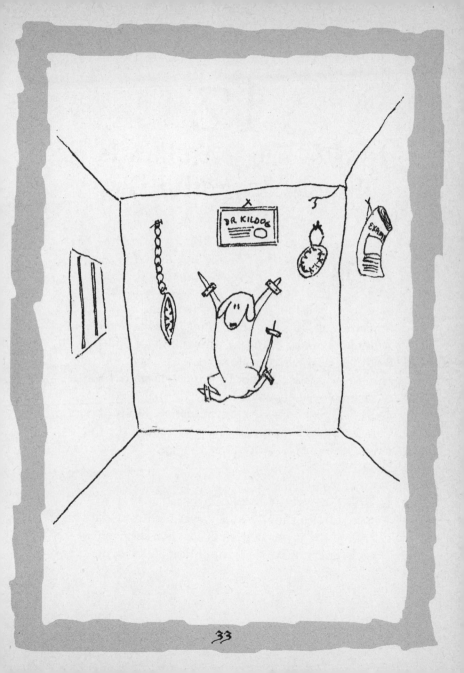

12

Master the Seven Habits of Highly Successful Dogs

eing a creature of habit, you will find that many habits listed here are instinctive or based on fundamental skills. (See *Everything I Need to Know I Learned in Obedience School*.) You will notice that the first three deal with facial expressions. The importance of mastering these cannot be overemphasized, because, when employed effectively, they will enable you to avoid discipline in almost any situation. Study these expressions. Then, practice them in front of the mirror when the owner is away.

1. Know When to Look Pathetic
(head angled slightly down, eyes turned upward toward the owner with a little white showing underneath; if possible, chin is leaning on something)

Case Study

You and the owner walk past a large mud hole. Unable to resist, you jump in. Within seconds, you are covered with foul-smelling mud. You wallow in the mud for several minutes, ignoring the owner's calls. When the owner starts becoming enraged (see chapter 14, "Read Your Owner Like a Book"), emerge from the mud hole and employ the Pathetic Look. This look says, "*Mea culpa, mea culpa, mea maxima culpa.*" You will escape punishment but may be unable to avoid the tub. (For more on guilt, see *When the Owner Says "No" I Feel Guilty*.)

2. Know When to Look Innocent
   (eyes wide open and trusting)

Case Study

You have just grabbed one end of the toilet paper roll and carried it joyously from the bathroom into every other room, leaving a trail throughout the house. As the owner realizes what you have done and starts getting red in the face, drop the toilet paper and immediately employ the Innocent Look. The Innocent Look says, "I thought you might need this in another room."

3. Know When to Look Stupid
(blank, cowlike stare)

Case Study

One evening while the owner is hosting a party, you realize you are thirsty. For some reason, the water in your dish is just not tempting, and no one is offering you a gin and tonic. You walk into the bathroom and start drinking from the toilet. Within minutes, you realize the owner is standing behind you, hands on hips, thoroughly annoyed. (For insight into this behavior, see *Why Owners Are the Way They Are*.) Remain facing the toilet, but turn your head back toward the owner. Stare blankly, letting a little water drip from your mouth. The Stupid Look says, "Look, I'm a dog. Deal with it." (The owner always does.)

4. Know When to Shut Up

We all enjoy a little random, senseless barking from time to time. The danger here is that, in our enthusiasm, we may enter an uncontrollable 2-to-3-hour barking jag. If you feel this is a realistic possibility, try to start early in the evening. Barking throughout the early morning hours—or through "Nightline"— is a serious faux paw that could have you exiled from the neighborhood.

5. Sleep Only on the Bed

If you aren't already sleeping in bed with the owner, follow this simple two-step program: **(1)** Get onto the bed, and **(2)** capture the prime position.

Step One

Timing is important. Do *not* throw yourself onto the bed as soon as the owner approaches. Wait until the owner is tucked comfortably under the covers watching TV and getting sleepy. Then, with a confident air, spring onto the bed in a fluid, rapid motion as though this were the most natural thing in the world—as if to say, "Where did you *think* I was going to sleep?"

Step Two

If you have succeeded in getting this far, you will notice that you are not in the prime spot: the owner's spot.

Timing is crucial. There is a good chance the owner will visit the bathroom during the night. Once you are sure the owner is in the bathroom, creep into the owner's spot. Arrange your body so that it covers as much surface area as possible. (Small dogs need not despair: We have a dachshund friend, Ollie, who has learned to take up as much space in bed as a full-grown weimaraner.) When the owner returns from the bathroom, act unassuming. Of course you are sleeping in the owner's spot, but wasn't it understood that the owner was merely warming this spot up for you?

6. Practice the Principles of Power Sniffing

During walks, you will find that you can steer the owner practically anywhere you like by using the concept of Power Sniffing. If you take nothing else away from this chapter, remember this concept.

Power Sniffing is based on the principle that humans have a healthy respect for certain canine abilities, such as sniffing, which far outclass their own. When confronted

The power sniff

with intense ground-sniffing activity, the owner will assume you are tracking some very important scent and must be allowed to continue.

Here's how it works. Say you've been out walking and the owner turns to head home. You, on the other hand, have just spotted an attractive dog of the opposite sex and wish to continue in the same direction. Immediately lower your nose to the ground and begin to sniff, trotting in the direction of the sniff. The owner will follow blindly.

By using this concept properly, you will find the owner can be dragged just about anywhere. We have a bloodhound friend, Harvey, who dragged his owner clear across state lines using this method.

7. Wag Your Tail Even When You Don't Feel Like It

Sometimes, you will simply have a dog day. (See also *When Bad Things Happen to Good Dogs* or *When the Treats Run Out*.) When this happens, the best thing to do is wag your tail. Studies have shown that sometimes the mere act of wagging will make you feel better.

13

Face Your Fears

Small, Aggressive Dogs

*J*f you are a large dog who is terrified of small, aggressive dogs, don't despair. You are right to be terrified—small dogs have no fear. It's not just that they *show* no fear. Small dogs actually *have* no fear. Of anything. If small dogs could wear tattoos, they would. When a bichon frise meets a rottweiler in the elevator, you can bet that it's the rottweiler who looks up at the numbers to avoid eye contact. (Even small, aggressive dogs are afraid of small, aggressive dogs.)

Now, this is not because small dogs are malicious. It is simply a survival-of-the-species tactic. The bichon frise, which is small and fluffy and has a name that sounds a little like a dessert, knows that the rottweiler, which has been bred to Hunt Things, might be considering the bichon for dessert.

The best advice regarding small, aggressive dogs is this: Listen to your fear. Never attempt to stare down a small, aggressive dog. It could land you at the vet. (See below.)

The Vacuum Cleaner

The vacuum cleaner, on the other hand, is a stupid wimpy thing that is not to be feared. It sleeps in the closet all year. Every once in a while, before company arrives, the owner takes it out, plugs its tail into the wall, and pushes it around. It makes a lot of noise. Then, it is stuffed back into the closet without even getting any food. What kind of animal allows itself to be treated this way? Trust us: You have nothing to fear from the vacuum cleaner.

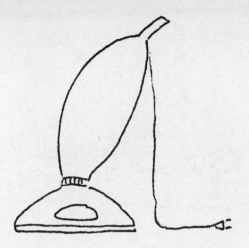

Humiliating Nicknames

Try to not become upset when the owner calls you various humiliating nicknames, such as "plum-brain," when the two of you are alone. Realize that this kind of name-calling says far more about the owner than about you. (Besides, you probably use a much greater percentage of your brain than she does.)

Cats

It is okay to fear the cat. Cats somehow manage to get food, toys, treats, comfy pillows, and the owner's undivided attention by doing absolutely nothing. This shows that cats have a Master Plan, and everyone should fear them.

The Vet

We tried to write about the vet but our paws started shaking too badly. Sorry.

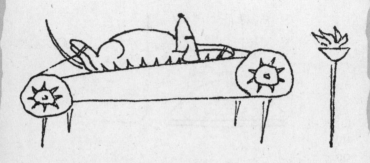

14

Read Your Owner
Like a Book

*W*e could spend pages here offering tips on interpreting human behavior, but in reality, there are only two situations we need concern ourselves with: **(1)** The Owner Is Mad, and **(2)** The Owner Is Very Mad.

1. The Owner Is Mad

The face is growing red, the hands are on the hips, and you hear the words "WHAT DID YOU DO?" (This is a rhetorical question—do *not* attempt to answer it.)

2. The Owner Is Very Mad

The same question is repeated, but the voice has risen an octave and the arms are gesticulating. Immediately employ the Pitiful Look, the Innocent Look, or the Stupid Look, depending on the circumstances. (See chapter 12, "Master the Seven Habits of Highly Successful Dogs.")

A final note here. While it is essential for you to develop these interpretive skills, you should never let owners feel they can read *you* like a book. It's a well-known fact that humans love mystery. (This explains their ongoing preoccupation with VCR programming, French New Wave cinema, and cats.) We, on the other hand, tend to be somewhat predictable. There are any number of ways to keep the owner guessing. Here are a few of our favorites (but the list is, of course, endless):

1. Pretend to hear a compelling noise that is not within human decibel range.
2. Sniff the owner's eyelid.
3. Stare at the owner out of the corner of your eye for a prolonged period of time.

If all else fails, bark in another language.

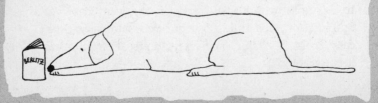

15

Use Body Language to Get What You Want

*I*f you've read *Owners Are from Mars, Dogs Are Called Pluto*, you know that effective communication between the species can be extremely difficult. Here are methods for correcting bad owner behavior and introducing positive owner conditioning in three important areas.

Food

You may find the owner is trying to feed you hard, dry dog food from a sack. Often, it is a pet-store brand advertised as being "packed with the special vitamins and nutrients a dog needs." When the owner offers you this food, no matter how hungry you are, *sniff at it once and walk away*. Several minutes later, wander back to the bowl disinterestedly and take a few mouthfuls. Spit at least one mouthful out, letting the pieces cascade to the floor with a hollow, clicking noise. Then, look at the owner, sigh, and walk away.

Remember, do *not* let the owner think you are interested in the food, no matter how enticing it may look or how hungry you may be. If you do this for three days in a row, you will find that the owner is soon mixing in wet food with the dry to try to tempt you. While the wet food amounts to progress, it is still not acceptable if it is dog food. Continue to appear uninterested.

If you practice this behavior faithfully, you will find that, within two weeks, the owner is beginning to cook for you—frequently chicken or meat dinners complete with gravy. The owner will be so delighted that you are eating that she will prepare special meals for you every night. But remember to be reasonable. If your owner is a hardworking career person, do not become upset by an occasional TV dinner.

Love

We all know of dogs who display wild enthusiasm whenever their owners arrive home. (See also *Dogs Who Lick Too Much*.) This is dangerous. By acting excited whenever the owner returns, you reinforce the notion that it is acceptable for the owner to return home at any hour—6 P.M., 7 P.M., 8 P.M., etc. After 7 P.M. on a weeknight is *not acceptable*. Practice the following behavior when the owner arrives home late:

1. Cultivate a look of "torpor": eyes three-quarters closed, body lying flat out on the ground, chin resting on the floor between the front paws.
2. Flash the owner a slightly suffering look, as if to say, "Oh, nice of you to stop by."
3. Rise to your feet slowly and wander over to the owner. (It is acceptable to wag the tail at this point, but not too rapidly.)

Note that it is important to remain polite when the owner arrives. Do not engage in destructive chewing to "punish" the owner. (See chapter 2, "Break the Cycle of Passive-Aggressive Chewing.")

If you play your cards right, you and the owner will be watching the six o'clock news together on a regular basis.

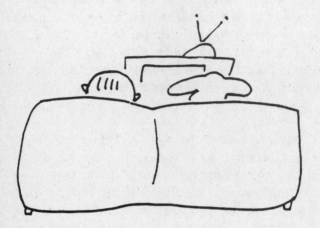

Heavy Petting

The key here is to remember that many owners are a little insecure in this area and need encouragement. When the owner approaches you for a petting session, help things along by **(1)** rolling over onto your back, **(2)** placing your paws in the air, and **(3)** closing your eyes halfway.

When the owner gets to a spot you like, begin moving your hind leg in a rapid circular motion. Owners seem to like this gesture—they interpret it as a sign that they are doing a good job. Don't worry if you have to fake it a little. The owner will get better and better with practice.

16
Use Every Waking Hour to Sleep

*I*f you're not sleeping at least 16 hours a day, you may have insomnia. Our friend Bubba, a Border collie, was having trouble sleeping. It took him years to realize that, as a herding dog, it simply wasn't effective for him to be counting sheep. If this sounds familiar, try counting something inanimate that defies herding, like potholes. If you find you *still* cannot sleep, try the following simple exercise:

1. Find a nice soft spot.
2. Circle around three times.
3. Plop down.
4. Turn on C–SPAN.

As a last resort, try a little rawhide dipped in cognac. Be careful, though. Unless you are an Australian cattle dog or your name is Duke, too much rawhide before bed has been known to cause nightmares.

17
Dare to Stare

ome of you may suffer from an inability to make or maintain eye contact when meeting other dogs. This is a potentially devastating problem as it bespeaks a lack of confidence that screams, "I'm a submissive breed." You must learn to make the other guy blink first.

Practice in front of the mirror. Look yourself in the eye and pretend you are staring at the toughest, meanest junkyard dog you've ever met (or a small, aggressive dog, for that matter.) Stare in a Robert De Niro *Taxi Driver* kind of way that says, "You talkin' ta me?" Or, if you prefer, in a Clint Eastwood way that says, "Feel lucky, punk?"

After you've practiced in front of the mirror for a while, move on to live objects. Start with the cat. (Yes, the cat counts as a live object.) Then, graduate to a human. (Any human will do, but you should try to avoid postal workers.) Once you feel you're ready for a dog, pick a gentle, friendly breed like a golden retriever or a Newfoundland. Walk up and make eye contact. Concentrate on maintaining the stare until he looks away. If you have a desperate urge to blink, suddenly bark at the other dog, "Hey! Isn't that a fire truck behind you?" You'll find that, nine times out of ten, the other dog will look away.

Sometimes, of course, discretion is the better part of valor.

Warning signs that it's time to look away:

1. The other dog's head is bigger than your whole body.
2. The other dog has not looked away after three hours.
3. The other dog is a small, aggressive dog.

18
Mark Only
What Counts

*I*t's only natural to want to make your mark in life. After all, you probably grew up with your parents telling you things like "Aim high" and "Shoot for the stars." The problem is that, in attempting to mark everything in sight, we often end up losing more ground than we gain.

Case Study

How many times has this happened to you: You're out walking with the owner, enthusiastically marking everything in sight. A tree here, a shrub there, a lamp-post on the corner. You're in rare form. Suddenly, you come to something *really* worth marking—say, an historical landmark or, possibly, a Harley-Davidson.[1] But, try as you may, you find you're able to do little more than "go through the motions." You end the walk feel-

---

[1] Under no circumstances should you attempt to mark a Harley-Davidson if its owner is sitting on top or is anywhere in the vicinity.

ing dissatisfied and inadequate, sensing the true "prize" has eluded you.

Contrary to popular belief, drinking more water is no solution. To really succeed, you must shed the limiting notion that marking more things will make you happier. In fact, the opposite is true. Consider the Labrador who marks the fence post. He may *think* the fence post is his, but is it really? He goes home and spends the rest of the evening worrying about the mastiff or the greyhound who may come after him.

The key here is that you must learn to be less possessive. The next time you're out walking with the owner and the urge to mark arises, stop for a minute and ask yourself: "Is this magazine stand *really* important? What if there is a fire hydrant or, better still, a Miata waiting just around the corner?" If you practice a little restraint, you will find yourself losing the urge to mark obsessively, and you will feel incredibly free. Suddenly, you will find yourself saying things like "I can let the German shepherd down the block have this Range Rover—I don't need it."

19
Practice Simulated Listening

imulated Listening is effective because it gives the appearance of genuine interest without your having to expend too much effort. When the owner begins talking, practice the following behavior:

1. Prick up your ears.
2. Tilt your head to one side.
3. Stare intently at the owner.

If the owner goes on for a long time, tilt your head to the other side and continue to stare. (Try to avoid yawning at the owner.) When the owner finishes, it is acceptable to walk away, but you should pause for a few seconds to give the effect that you are letting the words sink in.

Selective Listening

Be careful not to tune the owner out completely, as you should listen selectively for the following words and phrases:

- Treat
- Dinner
- Num-nums
- Treat
- Dinner
- Num-nums
- Wanna Go Out?

When used in combination with Simulated Listening, Selective Listening will enable you to tune in to only what is necessary. This frees the mind for quiet meditation.

20

Don't Scratch the Seven-Year Itch

*I*f you and the owner have been together for seven dog years, you are probably middle-aged. You may find that the owner is beginning to look a little humdrum. Suddenly, you're not racing to the door when she arrives home, and the way she talks baby talk to you (which you used to think was so cute) and calls you Mr. Sweet Paws is now a little nauseating. You may even find yourself entertaining fantasies about one of the owner's friends. *This is a big mistake.* You should never trade in an owner who loves you for a passing whiff of pheromones.

If you feel yourself growing bored, mark some new territory, cultivate a different odor, or chase your tail in the opposite direction. Do not scratch the seven-year itch or you will most certainly end up wearing the flea collar of despair.

A cautionary note: The itch may strike the owner as well. The sudden appearance of a birdcage or an aquarium is a warning sign. From there, it is a small step to the arrival of a puppy, or worse—a cat. Don't despair. There are several proven techniques for rekindling the relationship. The next time the owner comes home, greet her at the door wearing only a flea collar and a smile. Also, a dab of chocolate behind the ears has been known to work wonders.

21

Cope with the Unfaithful Owner

Which leads us to another disturbing issue. There may come the terrible moment when the owner returns home late at night with a cheerful expression on her face and the smell of another dog on her jeans. You may even see a few unfamiliar stray hairs on her clothing. As painful as this may be, be careful not to jump to conclusions. After all, the owner is entitled to have dog friends, and there is no reason to assume heavy petting or prolonged eye contact was involved.

If you are fairly certain, however, that the owner has become involved with another canine (say you have found biscuits—not your brand—in the owner's pocket), it is best to communicate your true feelings. Grab the offending items of clothing from the hamper and rip them to shreds. It may take a few outfits, but eventually the owner will get the point.

22
Get in Touch with Your Feminine Side

This pertains to large male junkyard dogs, dogs who work in police K-9 units, and guard dogs who answer to the name Spike and may be seen wearing studded leather collars. Our advice to you is simple: It's okay to shed the macho image. Ear cropping is out. Beef-flavored mineral water is in.

It's okay to be submissive. You don't have to bare your teeth every time you meet a strange dog. It's okay to have your belly scratched. It's even okay to like PBS dog specials.

Learn to slow down and smell the flowers. Next time you get home, instead of engaging in vicious barking, try a bubble bath and some biscotti.

23
Know Your Sign

*S*ome people say astrology is just so much mumbo jumbo, but we don't think so. You should learn your sign and be proud of it, just in case the stars are right.

Aries (March 21–April 19)
This is the most active, energetic sign. If you are a Jack Russell terrier—or any other dog who likes to bounce on and off the couch for hours on end—you are probably an Aries dog. Beware of owners who try to lace your Gaines.Burgers with Valium.

Taurus (April 20–May 20)
You are reliable, slow, and patient, and you never curse under your breath when the owner forgets where she put the leash. You tend to have a thick, heavy neck. An unusual number of bulldogs and bull terriers are born under this sign. Beware of owners who may ask

you for investment advice and then blame you if the market crashes.

Gemini *(May 21–June 21)*
You are intelligent and inquisitive but also jumpy and changeable. You have been known to hide under the bed during a thunderstorm or when the stock market takes a plunge. Many collies, Chihuahuas, and toy poodles are born under this sign. You're most comfortable when you and the owner are watching the Weather Channel.

Cancer *(June 21–July 22)*
You're sensitive, protective, and home-loving, but you're also fond of exploring and sniffing out secrets. Many of you are bloodhounds, basset hounds, and Great Danes. When the owner is away, you like to curl up by the fire with a good Agatha Christie or a true crime drama.

Leo *(July 23–August 22)*
You're lionlike, dominating, and fearless, and God help the dog who tries to take away your rawhide chewie. You are likely to have a fine head of hair and a short snout. Many terriers are born under this sign. Beware of bigger dogs with bigger snouts.

Virgo *(August 23–September 22)*
Intelligent and reliable but sometimes a bit fussy, you're a finicky eater and the sign most likely to have the owner cooking gourmet dinners for you. Yorkies,

Pekingeses, and Malteses are frequently Virgos. You may fly off the handle if the owner substitutes tofu for meat in your beef Wellington.

Libra (September 23–October 23)

You're typically well-adjusted and good at creating harmony around you. You have a pleasing, balanced nature and are likely to have a cheerful name like "Bucky." When the owner forgets where she put the leash, you sit amiably—often slobbering a little—and wait for her to find it. A good many golden retrievers and, of course, mixed-breeds are Libras. Beware of owners who like to watch professional hockey.

Scorpio (October 24–November 21)

You have strong willpower and a sharp, resilient mind. When the owner forgets where she put the leash, you can usually figure out where it is within seconds and lead her to it. Many poodles, Labs, and German shepherds are born under this sign. You get mad when the owner throws out your Mensa newsletter.

Sagittarius (November 22–December 21)

You are fiery and imaginative but restless and easily distracted. You love the outdoors and hunting and like to run around a lot, although you are sometimes known to run into trees. Your response to most commands is, "Huh?" Many Irish setters are Sagittarians. You tend to chase cars with good bodies but bad engines.

Capricorn (December 22–January 19)

Solid and practical, you are a determined leader capable of butting away all obstacles. You have a bent for politics. You're convinced that in a past life you were FDR's Fala, Richard Nixon's Checkers, or one of LBJ's beagles.

Aquarius (January 20–February 18)

You have a strong individualistic (and uncannily human) streak that leads the owner to question whether you might not be the reincarnation of some deceased great-aunt or -uncle. As a result, you are the sign most likely to be named the sole beneficiary in the owner's will. Many standard poodles are Aquarians. You prefer to be adopted by eccentric California millionaires.

Pisces (February 19–March 20)

You're a natural swimmer and can't get enough of the water. (But you always wait at least 20 minutes after the last bowl of kibble.) Not surprisingly, many Newfoundlands, Labs, and other retrievers are born under this sign. You've been known to nap in the Jacuzzi while the owner is away.

24
Sniff the Career Path

*W*e all know plenty of type A personalities—Seeing Eye dogs, rescue dogs, dogs who go to hospitals and nursing homes to cheer up patients, and so on. While this kind of volunteer work is admirable, you should never feel guilty about doing simply nothing at all. Your job, after all, is to Sit and Look Cute.

If the owner absolutely *insists* that you work, however, be sure you don't end up in a dead-end job. There are good jobs and bad jobs.

Good Jobs

- Television sitcom/dog food commercial acting
- L.L. Bean catalog modeling
- Professional Frisbee catching
- Stud services

Bad Jobs

- Drug sniffing/bomb sniffing
- Sled pulling
- Airport security
- Medical research

Note: Beware of professions that pose occupational hazards. We know plenty of Saint Bernards who regularly drain the sherry from their rescue barrels and plenty of drug-sniffing shepherds who continue to sniff long after the suspect has been apprehended. Also, be wary of ownership by high-profile political figures, as you may end up being subpoenaed to testify before Congress.

25
Stamp Out Shopping–Induced Trauma

*I*f you suffer from Shopping-Induced Trauma (SIT) and the related Shopping-Triggered Anxiety Yelping (STAY), you are not alone. Studies have shown that at least 65 percent of all dogs (and 35 percent of men) will begin crying within 30 seconds after the owner disappears inside a store. If there is a sale going on, this can escalate into a full-blown Episode. Don't worry. There are proven methods of dealing with SIT and STAY.

First, you must face your fears and realize that they are groundless. Let's explore some of the most common fears associated with this syndrome.

1. *Fear that the owner will decide to move into the store for good, leaving you permanently on the sidewalk.* You have no cause for concern. Extensive research has shown that this has happened only once, in Bayonne, New Jersey, and that involved a Price Club store. In every other instance, the owner emerged eventually.

2. *Fear that the owner will purchase something hideously ugly.* As you well know, there are any number of ways to deal with hideously ugly merchandise (see precautions on decorative pillows in chapter 2, "Break the Cycle of Passive-Aggressive Chewing").

3. *Fear that the owner is shopping for a replacement dog.* First of all, unless you have recently done something Really Bad (see precautions on decorative pillows), it's highly unlikely the owner is shopping for a replacement dog. Second, unless the owner is in a Price Club with a pet department, she is highly unlikely to *find* a replacement dog. Third, let's face it: How could the owner possibly replace *you*?

The next time the owner goes into the store and leaves you tied outside, consider the following pleasant diversions:

1. Count the number of people who ignore the PUSH sign and repeatedly try to pull the door open.
2. Clear your mind and practice the ancient Chinese art of Tie Chew.
3. If it is after Labor Day, count the number of people inappropriately wearing white shoes.

But most important, next time you're tied up outside a store, *don't worry*. For all you know, the owner is buying something for you—or at least something you both can enjoy, like a new pair of Amalfi pumps.

26
Shake Off the Holiday Blues

*A*s we all know too well, the holidays can be a difficult time of the year.

The owner seems a little anxious, and she is away more often at night doing the thing she calls "shopping." (This does not, however, resemble the usual exercise of bringing home bags, trying on the things inside, making small noises of disgust, and leaving the house again with the bags.) During the holidays, the owner arrives home with boxes, which she wraps up and *hides*. Later, she takes them out and gives them to other people, who unwrap them and make small noises of approval.

If you attempt to help the owner by hiding a few boxes yourself, or attempt to save everyone a little time by tracking down the hidden boxes and unwrapping them yourself, the owner will become very angry. She will be equally ungrateful when you risk your own well-being by sampling the freshly roasted turkey to make sure it is free of harmful salmonella.

If you're feeling unappreciated and depressed during the holidays—or just plain fed up with being forced to pose for holiday photos wearing little velvet antlers—don't despair. There are any number of ways to lift your spirits. Here are just a few:

1. Gift-wrap the obnoxious child who has been screaming all morning.
2. Spike the eggnog when no one is looking.
3. Tie up the cat with mistletoe and see how long it takes for someone to notice.

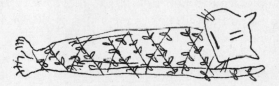

Note: While the list is limited only by your imagination, you should NEVER attempt to mark the Christmas tree. Our friend Carl, in Ohio, made this mistake and was never heard from again.

If all else fails, try a few hundred milligrams of Saint-Bernard's-wort.

27
Move without Misery

*B*eing creatures of habit, we naturally find it upsetting when the owner decides to move. Disturbing questions run through our minds, such as, "What if the dog next door has already marked all the good territory?" "What if I don't like the smell of the new place?" or worse still, "What if the owner forgets to change the address on my identification tag?"

Let's explore this last concern for a minute. If the owner *does* forget to change your ID tag and you get lost in the shuffle and end up at the wrong house, don't panic. Instead, look around and take stock. There might be a better deal here. Is this a one-VCR or a two-VCR household? Is there wall-to-wall carpeting? If there are decorative pillows, are they digestible?

Assuming, however, that you and the owner make it to the new home together, the first order of business is a thorough sniffing. You must determine whether other dogs have lived here before, and, more important, whether the house is haunted by the spirits of evil dogs.

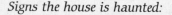

Signs the house is haunted:

1. The house is located on an ancient dog-bone burial site.
2. The rattle of choke chains echoes through the halls late at night.
3. Strange spots show up on the carpet and, for once, you have no idea how they got there.
4. The house screams, "GET OUT" (or, variously, "Get down," "Get off the furniture," or "Get my slippers").

If the house *is* haunted, don't worry. A simple technique for exorcising the spirit of an evil dog is to rattle a box of Milk-Bone biscuits outside the front door. Eventually, even the most determined spirit will be driven out.

28
Eat More Grass

*I*t is no coincidence that there is no such thing as a neurotic cow. Now, this is not because cows are particularly enlightened but because they have for years lived by a simple credo: You simply cannot eat too much grass.

While the digestive benefits of this herb are well known, we have recently discovered a whole host of new therapeutic uses:

Long, light-green blades	Enhance the sense of smell
Short, dark-green blades	Amplify the bark and improve the bite
Crabgrass	Intensifies natural odor
Lemongrass	Relieves stress
Oniongrass	Clears the sinuses (must be eaten in moderation)
Tall reeds	Instill a sense of peace and general well-being

Discover the health food store that is your own backyard. But first, a word of caution. If the owner has spent a lot of money on a lawn and garden expert, it is best to wait until the yard has been freshly mowed to sample the clippings. And remember—you should never eat the daisies.

29
Relax, Relax, Relax

*W*e've addressed many stress-relieving techniques throughout this book. Here are a few odds and ends we've neglected to mention.

Acupuncture. Rolling in pine needles is effective. (For shiatsu massage, simply substitute pinecones for pine needles.) Another good method is porcupine-wrestling, but you should proceed with caution here. Too much acupuncture can be a bad thing.

Aerobic exercise. If the owner does this at home with the women on TV, you can follow along. Everyone will start by stretching out. After a good long stretch, you can go back to sleep.

Hypnosis. This is especially good for kicking bad habits such as compulsive chewing. Simply stare at a spot on the wall. Keep staring until you fall asleep.

Soothing sounds. We've found some wonderful tapes to recommend. A few of our personal favorites are "Tumbling Milk-Bones," "Crashing Garbage Cans," and "Screeching Cats." Also effective are white-noise machines that provide a steady, soothing flow of sound. A good one will have multiple settings for chewing, scratching, and snoring. Check The Sharper Image.

Yoga. We recommend **(1)** the behind-the-ear scratch, **(2)** the infinite tail-chasing loop, and **(3)** the deep-sleep head tuck. These positions will enable you to achieve calmness and inner peace when you are between meals or naps.

The behind-the-ear scratch

30
Avoid Classic Time Wasters

*T*he point of this chapter is to learn to better manage our time. When it comes right down to it, there are only two essential activities in life—sleeping and eating (not necessarily in that order). Yet we waste precious moments on many nonessential activities. Here are some classic time wasters and ways to avoid them.

Begging. Use the three-minute rule. If you have been begging for three minutes without receiving even one potato chip, it is probably safe to assume the owner is going to be a greedy pig and finish the bag on her own. Give up and go back to sleep.

Chasing your tail. Again, the three-minute rule. If you don't catch it after three minutes, give up and go back to sleep. It will still be there when you wake up.

Playing fetch. The owner throws the ball. You chase the ball and bring it back. The owner throws the ball, you chase the ball and bring it back. Throw, chase. Throw, chase. The owner seems overjoyed with this. Just because the owner apparently doesn't have anything better to do with her time doesn't mean *you* don't. Three minutes max.

If you are unsure about whether a specific activity is essential or nonessential, refer to this handy chart.

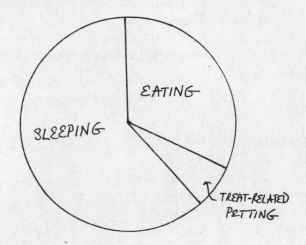

A final word here. It's okay to spend a few extra minutes a day letting the owner pat you on the head, especially if there's a chance this could lead to a treat. If no treat is produced, however, discontinue this practice.

31
Heel Thyself

Some people pooh-pooh home remedies, but we think they are important because, if practiced carefully, they may enable you to avoid a trip to the vet. Consider the following homeopathic cures for these common concerns:

Appetite loss	Sleep it off
Lethargy	Sleep it off
Headache	Sleep it off
Insomnia	Sleep it off
Ticks	Roll in the mud
Fleas	Roll in the mud
Mange	Roll in the mud
Dandruff	Roll in the mud
Obesity	Tell them to mind their own business

SPA

32
Love the One You're With

It is our sincere hope that you will be able to carry something away from this book. (Or maybe even the book itself.) But remember, life is unpredictable, and even if you are able to free yourself from many of the limiting beliefs and destructive behaviors we've discussed, you may still end up being spat at by the cat. If this happens, have a treat, curl up next to your owner, and take a nap.

About the Authors

MAX is a well-adjusted Lab mix of indeterminate age who is the author of numerous self-help books, including *Your Erroneous Bones*. He lives with his owner and translator, Liane Leshne, and her husband, Gary Blumenthal, in Washington, D.C. Liane is a lawyer and law journal editor-in-chief who enjoys writing, sketching, and playing the guitar. In her upcoming book, she will explore why Max always sides with Gary during family arguments.

SCOOTER is a thirteen-year-old AKC short-haired smooth dachshund who resides in Washington, D.C., with his co-owner/muse, Sharon Scott Armstrong. Scooter is a political animal who has overcome the stress of the city and found peace by using the techniques described within. Sharon is a human resources director who enjoys reading, painting, and spending time with her husband, Richard, when not "channelling" for Scooter.

Scooter was born in Johnstown, New York; Max's birthplace is "lost in history."